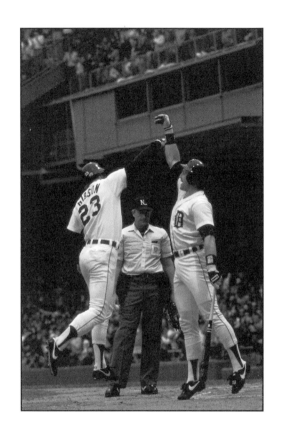

AL EAST

DETROIT TIGERS

ADMIT ONE

RICHARD RAMBECK

Published by Creative Education, Inc.

123 S. Broad Street, Mankato, Minnesota 56001

Art Director, Rita Marshall
Cover and title page design by Virginia Evans
Cover and title page illustration by Rob Day
Type set by FinalCopy Electronic Publishing
Book design by Rita Marshall

Photos by Allsport, Duomo, Focus on Sports,
Diane Johnson and UPI/Bettmann

Library of Congress Cataloging-in-Publication Data

Rambeck, Richard.

  Detroit Tigers / by Richard Rambeck.

  p.   cm.

  Summary: A team history of the Detroit Tigers, who
gave us Ty Cobb, Al Kaline, and nearly a century of
memories.

  ISBN 0-88682-447-8

  1. Detroit Tigers (Baseball team)—History—
Juvenile literature.   [1. Detroit Tigers (Baseball
team)—History.   2. Baseball—History.]   I. Title.
GV875.D6R36 1991   91-9491
796.357'64'0977434—dc20   CIP

THE HOME OF THE TIGERS

The city of Detroit, Michigan, got its start more than 250 years ago as a small frontier fort. It was located on a plot of land that connected two of the Great Lakes—Huron and Erie. In the 1800s Detroit became a key trading settlement, and the British and Americans fought to control it. In the 1900s the city became the automobile manufacturing center of the United States and grew into one of the largest metropolitan areas in the nation.

Detroit, which is on Lake St. Clair, near Lake Erie, is also a major international port. Goods are shipped from Detroit, through the Great Lakes, and up the St. Lawrence Seaway. Detroit is also served by ten railroads. In short, it is a hub of the midwestern United States.

The sweet swing of Ty Cobb.

In addition to its commerce, Detroit is known for a rich sports history. The oldest pro sports team in the "Motor City" is a major-league baseball club, the Detroit Tigers. When the American League was formed in 1901, Detroit was given a franchise. The new club was a success from the beginning, finishing third its inaugural season. The Tigers also placed third in 1905, the year an eighteen-year-old outfielder named Tyrus Raymond Cobb joined the team. Cobb would stay with the club for twenty-two years and would establish a standard for hitting that may never be equaled.

COBB LEAVES OPPONENTS FIT TO BE TIED

On his first trip to the plate as a Tiger, in a game against the New York Highlanders (later the New York Yankees), Cobb slammed a run-scoring double against Jack Chesbro, a pitcher who had won forty-one games in 1904. It was the first of 4,191 hits that Cobb would have in his major-league career, a record that stood until the mid-1980s, when Pete Rose broke it.

Cobb batted only .240 his first year, but it was the last time his average was less than .300. He won twelve American League batting titles in thirteen years, including nine in a row from 1907 to 1915. He hit more than .400 in 1911 and 1912. During Cobb's early years with the Tigers, the team was a consistent pennant winner or contender. Detroit, in fact, won the American League pennant three straight years, from 1907 to 1909, but lost in the World Series all three times.

Detroit was an exciting team, and Cobb was known as the best hitter in baseball. But opponents and some

Kirk Gibson's fierce desire reminded many of Ty Cobb.

The legendary Ty Cobb established a Tiger record by hitting safely in forty consecutive games.

sportswriters believed he was also a dirty player, someone who would sharpen the spikes on his baseball shoes and then go out of his way to try to gore the opposition with the spikes when sliding into bases. Cobb, though, denied this throughout his career. "It is untrue," Cobb said. "At no time did I use a file or any other sharp device. Not in front of the bench, nor anywhere else."

Cobb's sense of fair play may have been questioned, but his amazing ability to hit the ball where he wanted to never was. Before one game New York Yankee pitcher Urban Shocker was kidding Cobb while the Detroit star took batting practice. "Hey, Cobb," Shocker yelled. "Let's see you hit one to right." Cobb drilled a line drive down the right field line. Shocker then asked Cobb to do the same to left and then to center. Cobb obliged both times. Finally, as a joke, Shocker told Cobb, "Let's see you hit one into the dugout." Cobb lined the pitch into the Yankee dugout, and then slammed the next pitch right at Shocker, who had to scramble for safety.

Cobb was a remarkable player, and virtually everyone he came into contact with either liked or despised him. "No one, in any era, reached more people's emotions and influenced them the way the irresponsible Tyrus Raymond Cobb did," wrote Joe Falls in a history of the Detroit franchise. "When your own teammates will not talk to you and your own manager lets you set your own training rules, you have become quite an individual. . . . As there was only one George Herman "Babe" Ruth, there could be only one Tyrus Raymond Cobb."

Cobb, Sam Crawford, and Robert Veach keyed the Detroit attack, but they weren't able to produce a pennant for the Tigers after the team's success in 1909. When

Cobb, who also managed the Tigers for eight seasons during his playing career, finally left the team, in 1926, the Tigers had fallen on hard times. They finished no higher than fourth in the American League in the seven years after Cobb left. The fans, many of whom had lost much of their fortunes in the Great Depression, stopped coming to Detroit home games; in fact, the Tigers drew only 320,972 fans in 1933. At that point it was almost impossible to believe that success was only a year away, but it was, thanks to a catcher named Mickey Cochrane.

For the second consecutive season Charlie Gehringer was selected as a starter in the All-Star game.

Cochrane was sold to the Tigers by Philadelphia Athletics owner Connie Mack after the 1933 season. The price tag was $100,000, a fortune in those days, but Cochrane proved to be worth every penny. He not only caught for the Tigers, he was the team manager as well. Thanks to Cochrane's teachings, almost all of Detroit's top hitters improved in 1934. Hank Greenberg shed his image as an awkward, lumbering giant and batted .339 with 139 runs batted in. Charlie Gehringer hit .356, Cochrane .320, Marv Owen .317, Jo Jo White .313, and Goose Goslin .305. The pitching staff in the meantime, was led by Lynnwood "Schoolboy" Rowe. Rowe, who was only 7–4 in 1933, compiled an impressive 24–8 record in 1934 and won sixteen games in a row. Tommy Bridges, who was 14–12 in 1933, went 22–11 a year later.

The Detroit fans flocked to see the reborn Tigers, who won their first American League pennant in twenty-five years in 1934. Detroit's attendance almost tripled, to 919,161, as the Tigers finished the season with a record of 101–53. Detroit then lost to the St. Louis Cardinals four games to three in the World Series. The following year the Tigers staggered out of the gate at the start of the

9

Pitcher Doyle Alexander.

Shortstop Alan Trammell.

The secrets to the Tigers' success (L to R): Goose Goslin, Hank Greenberg, Charlie Gehringer.

season and were in last place in May. But led by Greenberg—who had thirty-six homers, 170 RBI, and a .328 average, and won the American League's Most Valuable Player Award—the Tigers rallied and eventually overtook the powerful New York Yankees to win another pennant. This time the Tigers won a seven-game World Series, beating the National League champion Cubs. The city of Detroit had its first World Series winner ever.

The Tigers remained one of the top teams in baseball for several years. The main reasons for their success were Greenberg, Rowe, Bridges, and Cochrane; unfortunately, the latter had to retire after being hit by a pitch in 1938. That same year Greenberg threatened to break Babe Ruth's single-season home-run record. The Detroit slugger slammed fifty-eight, only two behind Ruth's mark.

When Cochrane retired, Greenberg became Detroit's inspirational leader. Greenberg, who was named the American League's Most Valuable Player in 1940, carried the Tigers to American League pennants in 1940 and 1945. The 1945 team also claimed the World Series title, beating the Chicago Cubs four games to two.

Sadly for the Detroit fans, they would have to wait more than twenty years for the Tigers' next championship team. In fact, they would have to wait through a series of losing seasons. Stars such as Greenberg, Gehringer, Rowe, and Bridges soon retired, and the team's winning ways stopped. The Tigers still had some talented players, though, especially third baseman George Kell, who won the 1949 AL batting title, and pitcher Hal Newhouser, who retired in 1953 with two hundred career victories.

1 9 4 8

June 15: The first night game at Tiger Stadium was played as Detroit defeated the A's, 4–1.

KALINE IS ON-LINE RIGHT AWAY

The year Newhouser left was the same season Al Kaline joined the team. The eighteen-year-old Kaline went straight from high school to the majors. He never played an inning of minor-league ball. When he joined the Tigers in 1953, the youthful Kaline knew nothing about major-league baseball. He was scared and in awe of almost everything around him, especially manager Fred Hutchinson, a serious, gruff man who intimidated just about everyone. But Hutchinson took an interest in the youngster and told him to watch and learn as much as he could.

Kaline initially was used as a defensive replacement in the late innings. Although he played very little, Kaline

1 9 5 8

July 20: Detroit hurler Jim Bunning pitched a no-hitter in defeating Boston, 3–0.

expected nothing less than perfection from himself. In the ninth inning of one game, Kaline raced after a line drive and then dove, but didn't catch the ball. Two runs scored on the play, and the Tigers wound up losing by a run. After the game Kaline was extremely upset. "I thought I should have caught it because I was used to catching everything on the sandlots," he recalled later. "But they hit the ball a lot sharper in the major leagues, and I just couldn't reach the ball this time. Now I've got to go into the dressing room, and who's there next to me? Teddy Gray [the losing pitcher]. I'm sitting there, and I feel like crying. I really thought I should have had it. But before I knew it, he put his arm around my shoulder and said, 'Don't worry about it. You made a great effort. A lot of guys wouldn't have even tried for the ball.'"

It was that kind of effort that characterized Kaline's career. In addition to having a lot of hustle, Kaline was also an outstanding hitter. He won the American League batting title in 1955 when he was only twenty years old, making him the youngest player ever to lead either league in hitting. But Kaline didn't have much help from the rest of the Detroit lineup. The Detroit hitting attack consisted mostly of Kaline and Harvey Kuenn during the 1950s. Soon, however, the "K" boys would have some reinforcements.

Norm Cash, a first baseman, joined the team in 1960 and won the American League batting title a year later with a .361 average. Then, catcher Bill Freehan became a Tiger in 1961. In 1963 the Detroit roster was improved further by the additions of slugging outfielder Willie Horton and pitchers Mickey Lolich and Denny McLain. Finally, utility player Mickey Stanley arrived in 1964. The

In the footsteps of Kaline, first baseman Cecil Fielder.

For the thirteenth consecutive season Al Kaline (right) was selected to the AL All-Star team.

Tigers now had the talent of a championship team, but bad luck haunted them. They nearly won the 1967 American League pennant, but faded near the end of the season. In the season's final game, they needed a victory over the California Angels to force a playoff for the pennant with the Boston Red Sox. Detroit's pitching failed, however, and the Angels won 8–5. The loss was disappointing, and many people in baseball were unhappy for Al Kaline, who'd been with the team fifteen years and had never played in a World Series.

"It's not an obsession with me," Kaline said of playing in a World Series. "I know the players felt we had the best team and should have won the pennant. One game doesn't mean that much. We had 162 games to do it, and we didn't. It's been a tremendous experience for the guys on this team who'll be back next year."

Pitcher Mickey Lolich.

Unlike Kaline, Chet Lemon played in the World Series

Tiger pitcher Denny McLain (right) had a season unequaled by any pitcher in the modern era.

The wise veteran was right; the Tigers did learn from their near miss in 1967. Despite several key injuries during the 1968 season, the team jumped to the top of the American League. One of the injuries was suffered by Al Kaline, who missed much of the season as a result. The Tigers, however, remained in first place. This was mostly due to the amazing pitching of Denny McLain, who became the first major-league pitcher in thirty-four years to win thirty games, a feat no major-leaguer has accomplished since.

McLain actually wound up the season with a record of 31–6 with a 1.96 earned-run average. He was given both the Cy Young Award and the Most Valuable Player Award in the American League for his performance. But McLain wasn't the only Tiger who had a great year in 1968. Willie Horton slugged thirty-six home runs, Norm

Cash and Bill Freehan each had twenty-five, and outfielder Jim Northrup added twenty-one. Freehan and outfielder Mickey Stanley each won Gold Glove awards for their fielding; Stanley, in fact, didn't make a single error in center field all season.

Thanks to these heroics, the Tigers won a franchise-record 103 games to claim their first pennant in twenty-three years. In the World Series, the Tigers fell behind the St. Louis Cardinals three games to one as their ace, McLain, was beaten twice by St. Louis fireballer Bob Gibson. The Tigers rallied to win game five behind Mickey Lolich, who won his second game of the series, and Kaline, who drove in the winning run in a 5–3 victory. McLain won game six in St. Louis 13–1, setting up a decisive showdown in game seven, also in St. Louis. It pitted Gibson against Lolich, both of whom had already won two games in the series. The potbellied Lolich proved to be the best in this matchup. He pitched a masterful game as the Tigers won 4–1. Lolich, who became only the twelfth pitcher to win three games in a World Series, was named MVP. "I guess I'm an unlikely hero," Lolich said.

Kaline also was an unlikely hero. Hurt much of the season, he was a starter in the series only because Detroit manager Mayo Smith had shuffled his lineup, moving Northrup from right field to center field, and Stanley from center to shortstop. This switch allowed Kaline to play right field. He responded by batting .379 with eleven hits and eight RBI during the series.

Kaline played six more years for the Tigers, retiring after the 1974 season with 3,007 hits, 399 homers, and a lifetime batting average of .297. After Kaline retired, the

1 9 7 2

In only his second season as the Tigers' manager, Billy Martin leads the team to the AL East division title.

21

Tiger ace Jack Morris.

Tigers ceased to be one of the top teams in the American League East Division, which was formed in 1969 when the league was split in half. Pitcher Mark "The Bird" Fidrych charmed Detroit fans in the mid-1970s with his antics on the mound, including talking to the baseball and taking long walks between pitches. But Fidrych's career soon fizzled out. By the beginning of the 1980s, the Tigers had a new manager, George "Sparky" Anderson, who had built the fabulous Cincinnati Reds teams of the 1970s. The Tigers also had a new set of stars, the best of whom was a pitcher named Jack Morris.

1 9 7 6

Mark Fidyrch became only the second rookie pitcher in history to start in the All-Star Game.

MORRIS MASTERS THE FORKBALL

During the early 1980s, perhaps no pitcher in baseball was as dominant as Detroit right-hander Jack Morris. The Detroit pitcher was an occasionally hot-headed competitor who wouldn't settle for second best. "Jack has such high expectations of himself that when he doesn't live up to them, he shows it—in public," said Detroit pitching coach Roger Craig.

Craig spent a lot of time with Morris and taught the Detroit hurler the pitch that made him one of the best in baseball—the forkball. A forkball is thrown with the same motion as a fastball, but because the index and middle fingers are spread out when the pitcher grips the ball, the pitch drops just as it reaches the batter. Some have described a well-thrown forkball as a pitch that looks as if the bottom falls out of it. Few pitchers have mastered the forkball the way Morris did. "He always was an outstanding pitcher with the fastball," said Tom Paciorek of the Chicago White Sox. "With the forkball,

Left to right: Mike Henneman, Jeff Robinson, Lou Whitaker, Jack Morris.

he's a great pitcher. I don't think anybody in baseball is more talented than Jack Morris."

In 1984 no team in baseball was as talented as the Detroit Tigers. The team won thirty-five of its first forty games. Morris won ten of his first eleven decisions, including a no-hitter against the Chicago White Sox, the first thrown by a Detroit pitcher in twenty-six years. But Morris wasn't even the best pitcher on the Detroit staff in 1984. Relief pitcher Guillermo "Willie" Hernandez won both the Cy Young Award and MVP honors in the American League. In addition, starting pitchers Morris, Dan Petry, and Milt Wilcox combined to win fifty-four games. Catcher Lance Parrish had thirty-three homers and ninety-eight RBI, and right fielder Kirk Gibson added twenty-seven home runs and ninety-one RBI.

1 9 8 4

Sparky Anderson became the first manager to win the World Series in both the AL and NL.

Led by these performances, the Tigers were in first place in the American League East every day of the 1984 season, finishing with a 104–58 record. They then swept the Kansas City Royals in the American League Championship Series and defeated the San Diego Padres four games to one to claim their first World Series title since 1968. The MVP of the series was Detroit shortstop Alan Trammell, who had quietly become one of the best players in baseball.

THE EXPERTS DON'T SELL TRAMMELL SHORT

Trammell was hurt quite a bit in 1984, but he was healthy when it really mattered—during the World Series. In the years that followed, Trammell would rise above his injuries to become one of the most consistent players in the game. "I've always liked Trammell," said

Talented infielder Travis Fryman (pages 26–27).

Catcher Matt Nokes was selected to the All-Star Game and was the AL's Rookie of the Year.

St. Louis manager Whitey Herzog. "I thought he was as good defensively as anybody I'd ever seen."

Trammell also became a consistent hitter, one who tried not to do things he was incapable of doing. "You've got to know your limitations," he said. "I know I'm not going to hit thirty home runs a season. But I can hit double figures, ten or fifteen, and that's good enough."

Trammell and the Tigers proved to be good enough in 1987. Detroit was in second place in the American League East behind the Toronto Blue Jays during the final weeks of the season. But led by Trammell, second baseman Lou Whitaker, catcher Matt Nokes, and pitchers Jack Morris and Doyle Alexander, the Tigers caught the Blue Jays and won the division title. Although Detroit went on to lose to the Minnesota Twins in the American League Championship Series, it was a remarkable year for Trammell, who wound up second in the voting for league MVP.

Despite Trammell's continued success, the Tigers slumped to last place in the division in 1989 after finishing second in 1988. As the club prepared for the 1990s, manager Sparky Anderson knew he needed to unearth some new talent. Detroit found a gem of a player in Japan, where slugging first baseman Cecil Fielder had gone to play after failing to crack the Toronto Blue Jays' starting lineup. "When I went over to Japan, I didn't expect to come back for a long time," Fielder said. But after hitting thirty-eight homers for the Hanshin Tigers in 1989, Fielder signed a two-year, $3-million contract with Detroit.

Fielder continued his power surge in the American League, immediately rocketing to the top of the home-

The Tigers with the help of Lloyd Moseby (left), Rob Deer and Pete Incaviglia were vastly improved.

run charts. "Everybody knew he had the power," said Gordon Ash, Toronto's assistant general manager. "The question was how much was he going to play. Cecil struck us as the type of player who could achieve his maximum potential with everyday play. But we couldn't give him that." The Tigers could, however, and Fielder responded by leading the American League with 51 homers.

In addition to Fielder, the Tigers also picked up quality players such as center fielder Lloyd Moseby from Toronto, outfielder/designated hitter Larry Sheets from Baltimore, and pitcher Dan Petry from California. The team was so impressed with young catcher Mark Salas and veteran catcher Mike Heath that Matt Nokes, thought by many to be a rising star at the catcher position, was traded to the New York Yankees. Another young player,

Pitcher Dan Petry.

Second baseman Lou Whitaker.

third baseman Travis Fryman, worked his way into the starting lineup and seems on track to become a star of the future.

Detroit's personnel moves paid off, as the team went from embarrassment in 1989 to respectability in 1991. With Anderson, who is considered one of the best managers in baseball, and a group of veterans who know what it's like to win it all, the Tigers are optimistic the early part of this decade will be successful for the franchise that has produced Ty Cobb, Al Kaline, and nearly a century of great memories.